Tabby Cats

ABDO
Publishing Company

A Buddy Book
by
Julie Murray

VISIT US AT
www.abdopub.com

Published by Buddy Books, an imprint of ABDO Publishing Company, 4940 Viking Drive, Suite 622, Edina, Minnesota 55435. Copyright © 2003 by Abdo Consulting Group, Inc. International copyrights reserved in all countries. No part of this book may be reproduced in any form without written permission from the publisher.

Printed in the United States.

Edited by: Christy DeVillier
Contributing Editors: Matt Ray, Michael P. Goecke
Graphic Design: Maria Hosley
Image Research: Deborah Coldiron
Cover Photograph: Eyewire Inc.
Interior Photographs: Corel Images, DeVillier, Eyewire Inc., Getty Images, PhotoDisk Inc.

Library of Congress Cataloging-in-Publication Data

Murray, Julie, 1969-
 Tabby cats / Julie Murray.
     p. cm. — (Animal kingdom)
 Summary: Briefly describes the characteristics of the five types of tabby cat.
 ISBN 1-57765-645-8
     1. Tabby cats—Juvenile literature. [1. Tabby cats. 2. Cats.] I. Title. II. Animal kingdom (Edina, Minn.)

SF449.T32 M87 2002
636.8'22—dc21

                                                    2001046118

 KGW ntents

Domestic Cats

Thousands of years ago, all cats were wild. The Egyptians were the first people to tame cats. They brought cats indoors to kill rats and other pests.

Today, people around the world keep cats as pets. And these **domestic cats** are still the hunters they used to be. Domestic cats will kill mice, birds, and other small animals.

Domestic cats have not lost their hunting skills.

Colors And Markings

Like wild cats, **domestic cats** have different colors and markings. Some colors and markings help cats hide in trees or tall grass. This is called **camouflage.** Camouflage is useful when cats are hunting.

Spots, stripes, and **blotches** are the markings of a tabby cat. Tabby markings can look a lot like a wild cat's markings.

Wild bobcat

Domestic tabby cat

Tabby Cats

Many **breeds** of cats have tabby markings. There are Persian tabbies, Himalayan tabbies, American shorthair tabbies, and others. Many cats of no special breed are tabbies, too.

Tabby cats can be red, gray, silver, brown, or cream. Tabby cats can have long hair or short hair. Tabby markings are harder to see on long-haired cats.

Tabby cats have a special mark on their foreheads. This mark looks like the letter "M."

Classic Tabbies

Classic tabby cats have dark markings that are easy to see. Their shoulders and sides have **blotches** and circles. These are called butterfly marks. Classic tabbies also have striped tails. Rows of spots, or "buttons," mark their bellies.

Classic tabby cats

Mackerel Tabbies

Another tabby with easy-to-see markings is the mackerel tabby. This tabby has a dark stripe running along its back. Thinner stripes branch off from the bigger back stripe. These thin stripes look like fish bones. This is how the mackerel tabby got its name.

Mackerel tabbies also have "button" spots on their bellies. Their legs and tails have dark stripes. There are stripes called "necklaces" on the mackerel tabby's chest.

Mackerel tabbies have long, thin stripes.

Other Tabbies

Spotted tabbies look a lot like mackerel or classic tabbies. But they have spots instead of stripes. These tabbies also have "buttons" and "necklaces."

Spotted tabbies are not very common.

Tortoiseshell cats can be tabbies, too. Tortoiseshell cats commonly have red and black hair. Patched tabbies are tortoiseshell cats with tabby markings.

Ticked tabbies do not have a lot of spots or stripes. Instead, these cats have a lot of ticked hair. Each ticked hair has bands of dark color. Some Abyssinian cat **breeds** are ticked tabbies.

Can you see the bands of color on this ticked hair?

Ticked tabbies have fewer stripes.

Pet Tabbies

Tabby cats are common pets. Many people favor the American shorthair tabby. These cats are strong and healthy. They are friendly and get along well with children.

Tabbies make great pets.

Care

Cats are clean animals. They **groom** themselves by licking their fur. Cats often swallow hair as they groom. Brushing your cat removes the dead hair that could lead to **hair balls**.

Cats need food and fresh water every day. Follow the feeding directions on the cat food. Be careful not to feed your cat too much. Overweight cats can have health problems.

Some scratching posts have a sitting shelf on top.

Cats need something to scratch. You can buy a special scratching post for them. House cats also need a **litter box**. Clean your cat's litter box every day.

Kittens

Most tabby cats are born with their markings. These markings may get darker and clearer as kittens grow up.

As many as six kittens may be born in a **litter**. Newborn kittens are blind. After a few weeks, they can see. Kittens need their mother's milk. They should not leave their mother before they are 12 weeks old.

Fun Facts

- Cats can see in the dark six times better than people.

- Adult cats sleep about 16 hours each day.

- A purring cat is often happy. Yet, cats may purr when they are in pain, too.

- Adult cats have 30 teeth.

- A cat rubbing on your leg is marking you with its smell.

- Abraham Lincoln's son had a tabby cat.

- A cat's tongue feels rough because it has tiny spikes.

Important Words

blotches large spots of uncommon shapes.

breed a special group of cats. Cats of the same breed have the same markings.

camouflage when an animal's markings match the land around it. Camouflage helps an animal to hide.

domestic cats tame cats that make great pets.

groom to clean and care for.

hair ball hair that collects in a cat's stomach after grooming.

litter a group of kittens born at one time.

litter box a place for house cats to leave their waste.

Web Sites

I Love Cats.com

www.I-Love-Cats.com
Cat facts, games, pictures, and links to other cat sites can be found here.

The Cat Fanciers' Association

www.cfainc.org
Learn about the different breeds of cats.

Tabby Cat-SaSha Chan

www.geocities.com/sashachan/sasha1.html
Look up more information on tabby cats at this site.

Index